# MORE Classic Rhymes FOR Kiwi kids

Peter Millett and Scott Tulloch

Hickory Dickory Dock,
The kea nicked off with the clock.
The clock struck two,
The kea shot through,
Hickory Dickory Dock.

BEWAR
THIEVE

I'm a little fullback,
Short and stout.

Here is my haka,
Here is my shout.

When I see the try line,
Hear me spout:

‘Tip me over and
Stretch me out!’

One pukeko,
Two pukeko,
Three pukeko,
Four…

Five pukeko,
Six pukeko,
Seven pukeko,
More!

Itsy Bitsy spider
Climbed up the
Dunny spout.

Down flushed the
Drain and washed
Poor Itsy out..

Out in the sun, he dried himself again.
Then Itsy Bitsy spider climbed up the
Dunny chain!

Ten green geckos
Climbing up the wall.

Ten green geckos
Climbing up the wall.

And if ten green geckos should accidentally fall,

There'll be no green geckos climbing up the wall!

Pat-a-cake, pat-a-cake, Aunty Jan,
Bake me a pav as fast as you can.
Cut up some berries and juicy kiwi,
And we'll all demolish it right after tea!

Humpty Rugby sat on a goal.
Humpty Rugby fell off the pole.
All of the players
And ambulance men
Couldn't put Humpty together again.

Wee Willie Woolly skips through the town,
Upstairs and downstairs in his woolly gown.

Baa-ing at the windows and braying through the locks,
Crikey kids – it's time for bed – it's nearly nine o'clock!

Five Little Fielders standing in a row,
Three stood straight and two crouched low.
'Howzat?' cried the bowler,
And what do you think?

They all jumped up,
As quick as a wink.

Jack and Jill raced down the hill
And trail-biked through the water.
Jack let rip and pulled a flip,
And Jill came hooning after.

The eels in the tub go round and round,
Round and round, round and round.
The eels in the tub go round and round,
In the farmer's bath.

Little Bo-peep had naughty wee sheep,
And didn't know where to find them.
As quick as could be, she got a collie,
Who rounded them up behind her.

My old gran, she had fun,
She played lawn bowls in the sun.
With a click-clack near the jack,
Spinning really fast,
My gran's shot went rolling past!

Cobber, cobber, mend my shoe,
Get it fixed by half-past two.
Do it quick, and get it done!
She's up next at Riccarton.

Old MacDonald had a farm,
E-I-E-I-BRO.
And on that farm he had some grubs,
E-I-E-I-BRO.
With a huhu here and a huhu there,
Here a hu, there a hu, everywhere a huhu.
Old MacDonald had a farm,
E-I-E-I-BRO.

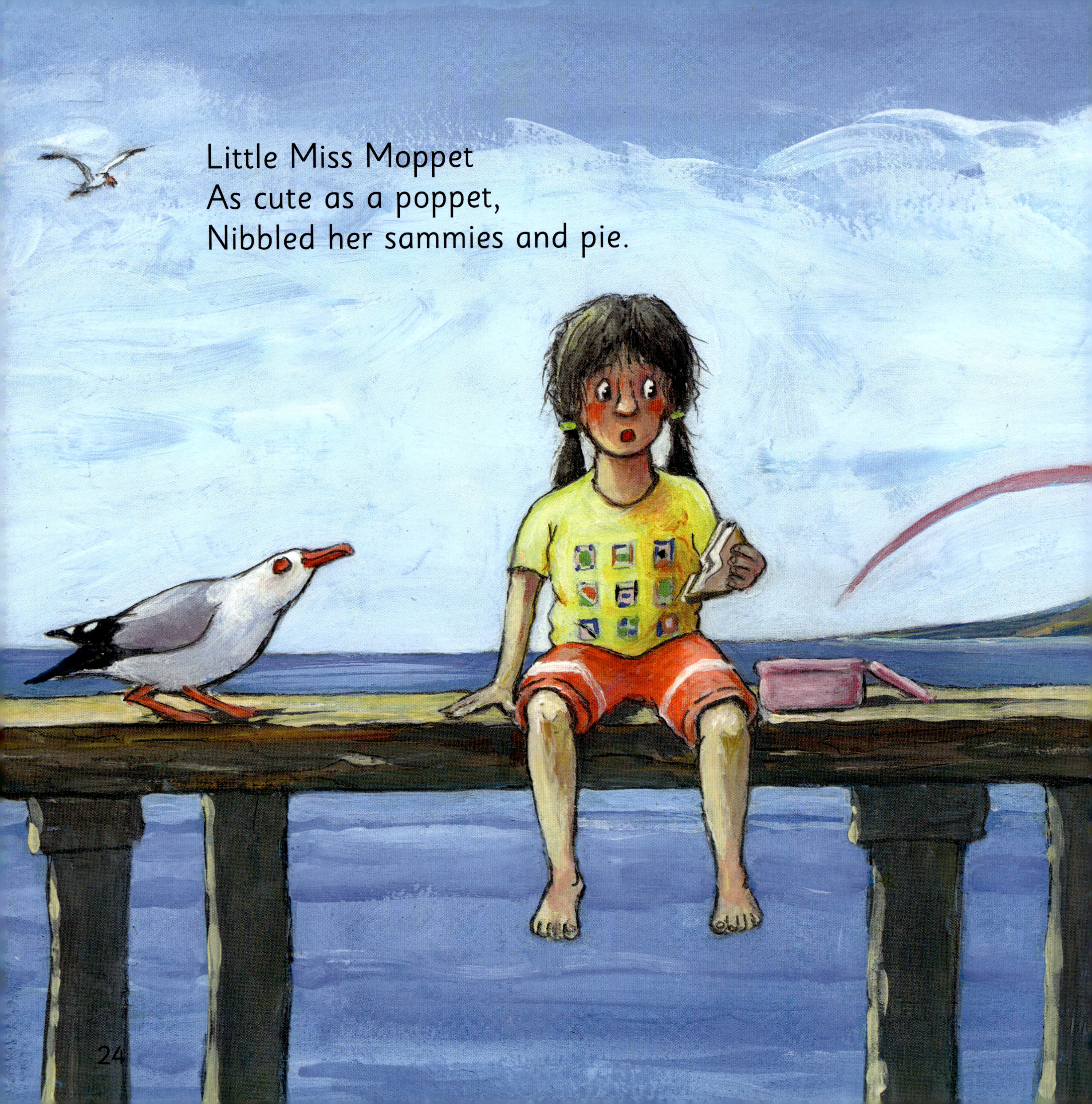

Little Miss Moppet
As cute as a poppet,
Nibbled her sammies and pie.

Along came a seagull,
Who took a big mouthful,
And gobbled up all of her kai!

Here is the Beehive,
It's full of MPs,
Buzzing around like noisy old bees.
Watch and you'll see them
Come out of the hive,
When the news is filming live!

Old King Cole scored a mighty fine goal,
And a merry old soul was he.
His last minute shot
Landed right on the spot,
And gave his team victory.

It's raining, it's pouring,
This holiday is boring.
We're stuck inside a leaky tent,
And we'll never get out 'til the morning.

Kiwi bird, kiwi bird,
Turn around.

Kiwi bird, kiwi bird,
Poke the ground.

Kiwi bird, kiwi bird,
Sniff for slugs.

Kiwi bird, kiwi bird,
Hunt for bugs.

Kiwi bird, kiwi bird,
Score a bite.

Kiwi bird, kiwi bird,
Say goodnight.

To Ruth, Geoffrey and Georgia. *PM*

To Zoe. *ST*

Published in 2018 by David Bateman Ltd
Unit 2/5 Workspace Drive, Hobsonville, Auckland 0618, New Zealand

Reprinted 2020, 2023

www.batemanbooks.co.nz

ISBN 978-1-86953-995-5



Book design: Alice Bell
Printed in China by Toppan Leefung Printing Ltd